Monographic Journals of the Near East   *Syro-Mesopotamian Studies* 1/4 (August 1977)

Terqa Preliminary Reports, N

A CUNEIFORM TABLET OF THE EARLY SECO

by

Giorgio Buccellati
Los Angeles

The single epigraphic find of the second season came from the surface, not far from one of the regular excavation units. It is a small administrative document of the same type as those from Mari dated to the period of the *šakkanakku*'s. Its importance lies in the inherent implications of (1) close links with Mari at that period, (2) well established archival procedures at Terqa earlier than known heretofore, and (3) possibly a special linguistic affiliation for Terqa in the early periods.

Table of Contents

1.   Archaeological Context

The tablet which is published here was found on the surface of the tell rather than in the course of regular excavations. Even though the find was made by accident, its location can be fixed with a certain degree of accuracy. As shown on the enclosed sketch map (Fig. 2), where the location is marked as SF1, the tablet came from the steep cliff cut into the northeastern side of the tell by the Euphrates; it was at an elevation of about one hundred meters north of SG4, the 1976 sounding where the remains of a private house were discovered. (A view of the location where the find was made is shown in slide No. 77A of the set *Audio-Visual Modules: Documentary Series* 1, Malibu 1977).

The find was made in the Spring of 1976 by Mr. Minnā Nijris, a resident of Ashara who is currently a student at the University of Damascus. He identified for us the place where he had found and picked up the tablet, and generously agreed to turn over the document for inclusion in our records. For his cooperation I wish to register here my sincere gratitude, especially because, as shown in the following pages, the scholarly importance of the tablet is considerable.

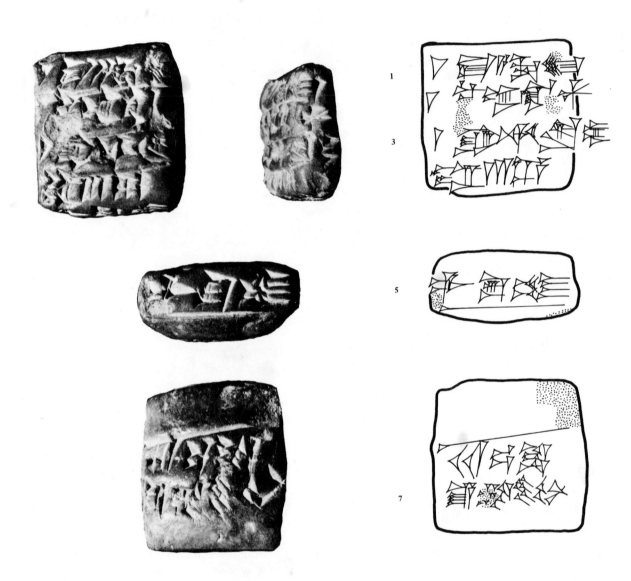

Figure 1. *TPR* 2 1: Photograph and Autograph Copy (1:1)

Similarly, I owe a special debt of gratitude of Mr. As'ad Maḥmud, Director of the Museum of Deir ez-Zor, who located Mr. Nijris and arranged for an official acquisition of the tablet on the part of the Syrian Directorate General of Antiquities.

Because of circumstances, the tablet was obtained only at the very end of the season, after we had already concluded our excavations and had started packing. As a result, it was impossible to probe the area where the tablet had been found. Such a probe could not, in any case, be very extensive because the findspot is only a few meters away from houses which are presently inhabited; nevertheless even a small test pit might be very informative, and it will be undertaken in the coming seasons. For now, our knowledge of the archaeo-logical context of the find is limited to the simple fact that the tablet was discovered at a relatively high elevation—in terms of absolute values, about four meters above the floor of the mid-second millennium house in SG4 (the sounding located about 100 meters to the southeast). Obviously, no stratigraphic conclusion can be drawn from a surface find, how-ever the excellent state of preservation of the tablet and the relative unimportance of its content may perhaps be taken to indicate that it had not been moved much in antiquity from its original place of deposition. If so—and it hardly needs stressing that this is purely a hypothesis—it may be that the early second millennium levels were higher toward the center of the mound than just one hundred meters to the southeast. But only a clarification of the stratigraphic context and, hopefully, the discovery of more tablets in the same location will allow us to pursue this argumentation.

The text has been inventoried in the Field Catalog under the number ASH2—T1, and is now housed in the Museum of Deir ez-Zor, Syria; the museum number is 1103.

2. Philological Presentation

A photograph and an autograph copy of the text are given in Fig. 1. (Two color slides of the tablet are also included as No. 76 and No. 77 of the set *Audio-Visual Modules: Documentary Series* 1, Malibu 1977). A transliteration, translation and commentary are appended below. For helpful suggestions in this section I am indebted to Professors I. J. Gelb, P. Michalowski and J. Sasson.

TPR 2 1

1	1 $^{\jmath}\dot{A}$-a-da-tu	1, $^{\jmath}$Ayya-dādu,
	1 $_{\llcorner}Ku_{\lrcorner}$-um-ra-an	1, Kumrān,
3	1 Ga-ti-ru-um	1, Kaddirum,
	ŠU.NIGÍN 3 GURUŠ	total: 3 workmen,
5	mar-ṣu-tum	sick;
	21 U$_4$ ITI	21st day, month of
7	E-bir$_5$ (NAM) -tim$_x$ (DIN)	Ebirtum.

Line 1. *$^{\jmath}$Ayya-dādu* "Where-is-the-beloved?" is an interpretation suggested by Gelb on the basis of the parallel attested in Mari as *A-ia-da-du* (*ARM* 7 269:8). The first element *$^{\jmath}$ayya* is attested in Old Akkadian (*MAD* 3, 2) as well as in Amorite personal names (Huffmon, *Amorite Personal Names*, p. 161). The same is true of the second element *dādum* (*MAD* 3,

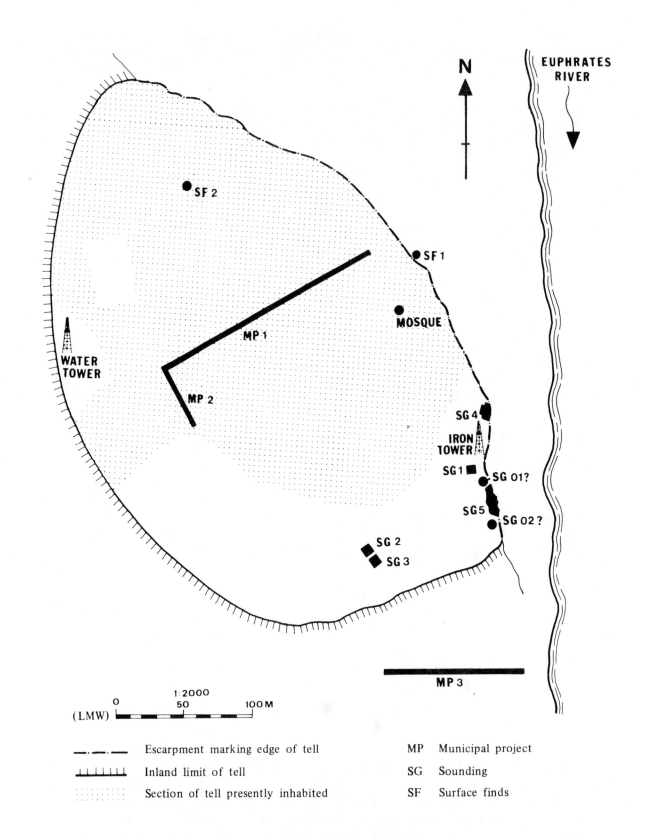

Figure 2. Sketch Plan of Ashara, Ancient Terqa.
SF1 marks the location where the tablet *TPR* 2 1 was found.

104; Buccellati, *Amorites,* p. 139, 185; Huffmon, p. 181f.). For the value ʾà for the sign É see *MAD* 2^2, p. 88f.; *ARM* 19, p. 6, 155. The writing with the sign TU is attested in *ITT* 4 7128 (*Da-tu-um,* quoted in *MAD* 3, 104), and this value of the sign is also attested elsewhere (*MAD* 2^2, 56). Lack of mimation is found in Old Akkadian personal names, cf. *MAD* 2^2, 145 (but see the remarks by I. J. Gelb, *RA* 50, 1956, p. 4). Another possible interpretation of the same name is to read the first element as the divine name Ea, thus yielding: "Ea-is-the-beloved."

Line 2. *Kumrān* is a hypocoristic of some such name as *Mu-tu-ku-um-ri* (*ARM* 10 166:13´) or *Ku-um-ri* (*RA* 65, 1971, p. 42, ii 59).

Line 3. For the third name I have no plausible explanation to offer. As a parallel, Gelb suggests *Ka-ti-ri* (*UET* 5 88:2). The transcription *Kaddirum* is proposed here only tentatively on the basis of Hebrew *kaddūr* "ball" and Arabic *kudur* "thick."

Line 5. The qualification "sick" occurs frequently in the texts published by Limet in *ARM* 19 (=*TCM* 3), where it appears once with a wrong grammatical agreement (2 MUNUS *mar-ṣum* instead of *marṣā,* 18:1-2; for the predicative dual 2 GURUŠ *mar-ṣ[a],* 55:12, cf. 57:1-2, see H. Limet, "Observations sur la grammaire des anciennes tablettes de Mari," *Syria* 52, 1975, p. 50; note also 1 GURUŠ *mar-<ṣum>,* 31:3). In the Mari texts the qualification appears either in the normal state (always in the masculine: *mar-ṣum*), or in the predicative state in the masculine or feminine: *mar-ṣa-at, mar-ṣa*); the context is identical in all instances, so that the difference in the use of the state does not seem to correspond to a difference in meaning. The Terqa text gives the plural masculine in the normal state, which is not found in the Mari texts.

Lines 6-7. The sequence 21 U_4 instead of U_4 21-KAM is typical of the Mari texts published in *ARM* 19. Also identical to those texts is the arrangement of the signs on two lines in such a way that the sign ITI is separated by line boundary from the month name which follows immediately. This is especially interesting since there seems to be a close nexus between ITI and the month name: the latter appears in fact often (as in our text) in the genitive, which implies that ITI stands for the construct state *waraḫ* (cf. Limet, *ARM* 19, p.12).

One more similarity between our text and the texts published in *ARM* 19 is to be found in the month name itself, which belongs to the Mari calendar (cf. Limet, *ARM* 19, p. 12). Since the month falls in the summer, its meaning may refer to the fact that the waters of the Euphrates are so low that the "crossing" or "wading" (*ebirtum*) of the river are easier than at any other time (differently from Limet, loc. cit.).

3. Historical Considerations

The chief importance of our text lies in its early date and its similarity with the Mari texts published in *ARM* 19. Some aspects of this similarity have been pointed out in the preceding sections—the use of the qualification "sick," the type of date formula, the month name. To these criteria one may also add those derived from graphemics and palaeography as well as from the overall structure of the text. With regard to the former one should note especially the use of the signs NAM and DIN in writing of the month name Ebirtum. As for palaeography there are similarities especially in the writing of the signs RU (l. 3), ṢU (l. 5), NAM

(l. 7), DIN (l. 7); slightly different, on the other hand, is the writing of the signs DA (l. 1), TU (l. 1), TUM (l. 5), UD (l. 6), ITI (l. 6; for a comparison with the Mari texts, check the list in *TCM* 3, pp. XIII-XX).

The similarity of the individual signs is further confirmed by the general similarity in the shape of the tablets and the nature of the ductus. For a verification of these relationships, I am much obliged to Prof. H. Limet who has very generously sent me photographs of some selected Mari tablets of the period of the šakkanakku's. Two of these (*TCM* 3 44 and 52) are reproduced here as Fig. 3: one can readily note, besides the practical identity of absolute dimensions, the great similarities in the profile of the tablet, the depth of the individual wedges (which tend to appear uniformly as elongated cones rather than as nails with a narrow body and a broad head), the general configuration of the signs in terms of the direction and orientation of the component elements.

The similarities, and the differences, in the structure of the texts may best be brought out by a comparative diagram of the key elements:

	ARM 19 1-102	*TPR* 2 1
(1)	–	personal names
(2)	n GURUŠ/MUNUS	total n GURUŠ
(3)	qualification	qualification
(4)	É.A	–
(5)	date	date

The Terqa text is more explicit in one respect, namely in that it refers specifically by name to the individuals concerned. The Mari texts are more explicit in another respect, namely in the definition of the transaction as one which concerns the outgo of (presumably) the rations for the individuals involved. Otherwise, the texts are practically identical, and they certainly seem to serve the same function within analogous archival and administrative systems.

It is on the basis of these close similarities that we can safely date the Terqa text to the same time as the texts of *ARM* 19, i.e. the period immediately following the end of Ur III, as argued conclusively by Gelb in 1956 (*RA* 50, pp. 1-10) and confirmed by the investigation of Limet (*ARM* 19, pp. 7-10, with references to earlier literature and a new discussion of the data). This makes of *TPR* 2 1 the earliest text to date found in Terqa.

Apart from the chronological question, the similarity between our text and the Mari texts of *ARM* 19 indicates a commonality of scribal tradition between Mari and Terqa already in the early periods. The nature of our text—an administrative record written for purely local purposes—is such that it can only be conceived as part of an archive and, more generally, as evidence of pervasive southern Mesopotamian influence. Whether more texts of the same, or of other, archives will be found in the future depends naturally on the vagaries of the process of cultural deposition through time and on the factor of chance which underlies the process of excavation. But even the evidence of a single text like this one has far-reaching implications in helping to characterize the nature of the earlier levels of Terqa as an urban settlement with an established bureaucratic system of personal accountability and permanent data recording, and all the necessary underlying scribal schooling which went with it.

Figure 3. Mari Texts of the Period of the Šakkanakku's (1:1).
(*TCM* 3 44 on left and *TCM* 3 52 on right.)
(Photographs courtesy H. Limet.)

Finally, our text allows also some interesting considerations with regard to linguistic affiliation of the people of Terqa at this period. In the first place, the personal names are Semitic, and possibly Amorite. Secondly, the pattern of the texts is such that it calls for the use of Semitic features next to the more formulaic Sumerograms. The Akkadian word *marṣūtum* "sick" is a good example of this, and if more texts are found of the same type we may look forward to more evidence about this early stage of Akkadian. Thirdly, since the Mari texts of *ARM* 19 are the only ones (together with the Mari liver models of the same period) to exhibit linguistic peculiarities similar to those of the Ebla texts (see especially Gelb, *SMS* 1/1, 1977, pp. 9-12), we may also expect that new Terqa texts of the same type might hopefully shed some light on this all important new dimension of ancient Near Eastern history.